Mc
Graw
Hill
Education

Cover and Title Page: Nathan Love

www.mheonline.com/readingwonders

Send all inquiries to:
McGraw-Hill Education
2 Penn Plaza
New York, NY 10121

ISBN: 978-0-02-132419-4
MHID: 0-02-132419-0

Printed in the United States of America

2 3 4 5 6 7 8 9 RMN 20 19 18 17 16

B

ELD
Companion Worktext

Program Authors

Diane August

Jana Echevarria

Josefina V. Tinajero

Mc
Graw
Hill
Education

Unit 1

Growing and Learning

Unit 1

Growing and Learning

The Big Idea

How can learning help us grow?

TALK ABOUT IT

Weekly Concept Storytime

? Essential Question

What can stories teach you?

>> *Go Digital*

4

COLLABORATE

Who is in the picture? What is she doing? Why is she laughing? Write words about stories in the web.

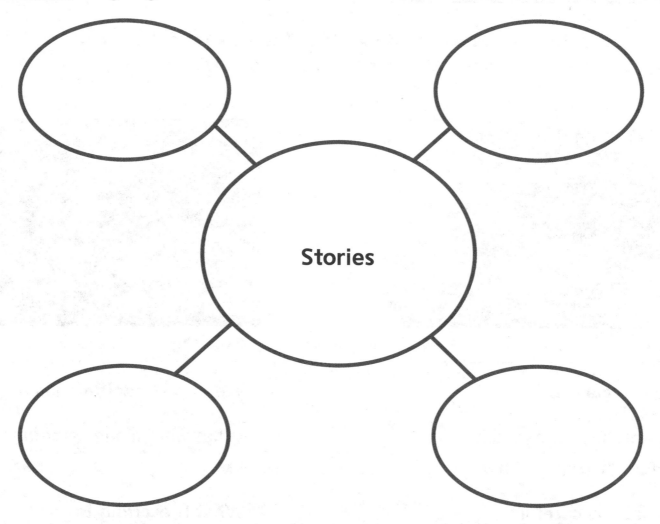

Stories

Talk about the girl. Use the words from the web.
You can say:

The girl is _____ a _____ .

The girl is laughing because _____ .

Books help the girl _____ new things.

More Vocabulary

Look at the picture and read the word. Then read the sentences. Talk about the word with a partner. Write your own sentence.

careful

The cook is **careful**.

What word means *careful*?

watchful   happy   big

When are you careful?

I am careful when I _____

_____

_____.

exciting

We won an **exciting** game.

What word means *exciting*?

sad   fun   bad

What is exciting to you?

_____

_____ is exciting.

Words and Phrases: *in* and *into*

The word *in* tells where.

Where is the boy?

The boy is **in** the car.

The word *into* shows motion.

Where is the girl going?

The girl is going **into** the van.

COLLABORATE

Talk with a partner. Look at the pictures. Read the sentences. Write the word that completes the sentence.

The bird is _____ the cage.
          in   into

The dog jumps _____ the pool.
          in   into

COLLABORATE

1 Talk About It

Look at the picture. Read the title. Discuss what you see. Use these words.

bear   cold   woods   leaves

Write about what you see.

The story is about _____

_____.

What is the bear's name?

The bear's name is _____.

Where does Bruno live?

Bruno lives in the _____

_____.

How does Bruno feel?

Bruno feels _____

_____.

Take notes as you read the text.

BRUNO'S NEW HOME

Essential Question

? **What can stories teach you?**

Read how a story teaches a bear a lesson.

Bruno **shivered**. His paws felt like ice. Winter was coming. Bruno needed a warm and safe place to sleep.

Bruno grumbled and growled. He was not happy. Finding a new place to sleep was hard.

Bruno walked in the woods. No place was right. Then he made an **exciting** discovery.

John Howell

① **Specific Vocabulary** Ⓐ Ⓒ Ⓣ

The word *shivered* means "to shake from cold." Read the first paragraph. Why does Bruno shiver? Underline the two details that tell you.

② **Comprehension**

Character

Reread the second paragraph. How does Bruno feel? Write the words that tell you.

_____

_____

③ **Sentence Structure** Ⓐ Ⓒ Ⓣ

Reread the last paragraph. The pronoun *he* refers to a character in the story. Who does *he* refer to? Circle the word.

Text Evidence

1 Specific Vocabulary ACT

The word *spotted* means "saw." What does Bruno spot? Write the word that tells what Bruno spots.

_____

2 Sentence Structure ACT

Reread the fourth paragraph. Look at the pronoun *they*. What does *they* refer to? Circle the word.

COLLABORATE

3 Talk About It

Why do Bruno's paws hurt?

Bruno's paws hurt because

_____.

Write two words that describe Bruno's paws.

_____

_____

Bruno **spotted** a cave. It was perfect. But there was one problem. Bruno could not go through the opening. A pile of dirt and tree roots blocked the hole.

Bruno said, "I will dig out this dirt. I will make the opening bigger."

Bruno dug and dug, but the dirt was too hard. He pulled at the tree roots.

The roots were very strong. Bruno stopped to rest. His paws ached. They were red and sore. Then he heard a loud sound.

Bruno saw a small squirrel. The squirrel was eating a nut.

The squirrel asked, "Do you need help?"

Bruno sighed. "I cannot fit into this cave. I dug and I dug. But it is hopeless. The opening is still too small."

"I am Jack. I can help you," said the squirrel.

"You are too small," said Bruno. "You cannot help me."

Jack told Bruno to sit. Then Jack scampered away. A few minutes later, Jack came back.

John Howell

1 Comprehension

Reread the third paragraph. Why does Bruno need help?

Bruno needs help because

_____.

COLLABORATE

2 Talk About It

Does Bruno think Jack can help? Circle the sentence that tells you what Bruno thinks.

Do you agree with Bruno?

Justify your answer. _____

_____

_____.

3 Specific Vocabulary A C T

The word *scamper* means "to run quickly." Who scampers away?

_____

Text Evidence

1 Sentence Structure **A**C**T**

Reread the first paragraph. Circle the quotation marks. What words does Jack say to Bruno? Underline the words.

2 Specific Vocabulary **A**C**T**

Look at the word *bright* in the second paragraph. Circle the word that has almost the same meaning.

COLLABORATE

3 Talk About It

Jack asks Bruno to read a story. The story is about a lion and a mouse.

Why is Jack like the mouse?

Jack is like the mouse because

_____.

Why is Bruno like the lion?

Bruno is like the lion because

_____.

Jack gave Bruno a book. "Read this book," said Jack.

Bruno moved to a **bright**, sunny spot to read. He paid **careful** attention to the story.

The story was about a lion and a mouse. The lion thought the mouse was too small to help him. One day the lion got caught in a net. The mouse chewed the net's ropes and helped the lion escape.

"The lion learned an important lesson," said Bruno. "I learned a lesson, too."

Then Bruno had an idea. The mouse had sharp teeth. Jack had sharp teeth, too. Jack could help Bruno.

The new friends worked together. Jack chewed through the thick roots. Bruno dug out the dirt. Finally, Bruno was able to walk through the opening.

"Are you happy with your new home?" asked Jack.

"I am happy!" said Bruno. "And I learned something, too. Good friends come in small packages."

Make Connections

? Talk about the story of the lion and the mouse. How does the story help Bruno solve his problem? ESSENTIAL QUESTION

Discuss how you and your friends help one another. TEXT TO SELF

Text Evidence

1 Comprehension
Character

What kind of teeth does Jack have? Circle the word that describes Jack's teeth. Rewrite the sentence.

Jack has _____.

2 Sentence Structure Ⓐ Ⓒ Ⓣ

Reread the third paragraph. Underline the words *new friends* in the first sentence. Circle the words in the paragraph that tell who the new friends are.

COLLABORATE

3 Talk About It

What lesson does Bruno learn?

Bruno learns that _____

_____.

What is the small package?

_____ is the small package.

13

Respond to the Text

Partner Discussion Work with a partner. Read the questions about "Bruno's New Home." Show where you found text evidence. Write the page numbers. Then discuss what you learned.

What is Bruno's problem?

I read that Bruno needs _____.

In the story, Bruno finds a _____ but _____

_____.

The author writes that Bruno's paws _____.

Text Evidence 🔍

Page(s): _____

Page(s): _____

Page(s): _____

How does Jack help Bruno?

Bruno thinks Jack is too _____ to help.

In the story, Jack tells Bruno to read _____.

The author writes that Jack can help because _____

_____.

Text Evidence 🔍

Page(s): _____

Page(s): _____

Page(s): _____

Group Discussion Present your answers to the group. Cite text evidence for your ideas. Listen to and discuss the group's opinions.

COLLABORATE

Write Work with a partner. Look at your notes about "Bruno's New Home." Write your answer to the Essential Question. Use text evidence to support your answer. Use vocabulary words in your writing.

What does Bruno learn from the story he reads?

In the beginning, Bruno needs _____

_____.

Bruno does not think Jack can help because _____

_____.

Jack gives Bruno a book about _____.

The book teaches Bruno that _____

_____.

COLLABORATE

Share Writing Present your writing to the class. Discuss their opinions. Talk about their ideas. Explain why you agree or disagree with their ideas. You can say:

I agree with _____.

That's a good comment, but _____.

Write to Sources

pages 8–13

Take Notes About the Text I took notes about the story on this chart. I will respond to the prompt: *Write a paragraph. Add to the story. Tell how Bruno thanks Jack. Tell why Bruno likes Jack.*

Alicia

Bruno found a cave for a winter home.

↓

Roots blocked the opening.

↓

Jack chewed through the roots.

↓

Bruno walked into his new home.

Write About the Text I wrote a descriptive paragraph. It tells how Bruno thanks Jack.

Jack helped Bruno. Bruno was happy. Bruno thanked Jack. Bruno hugged Jack.

Bruno said, "I like you, Jack. You chewed through the roots. You helped me. Now I have a new home."

TALK ABOUT IT

COLLABORATE

Text Evidence

Circle words that tell why Bruno thanks Jack. What event does Alicia tell about?

Grammar

Underline a past tense verb. Why does Alicia use past tense verbs?

Connect Ideas

Draw a box around the first two sentences. How can you use the word *and* to connect ideas in the sentences?

Your Turn

COLLABORATE

Add a paragraph to the end of the story. Describe Bruno's new home.

>> Go Digital
Write your response online. Use your editing checklist.

17

? **Essential Question**
What can traditions teach
you about cultures?

>> *Go Digital*

COLLABORATE

Who is in this picture? What is she doing? What is she weraring? Write the tradition words in the web.

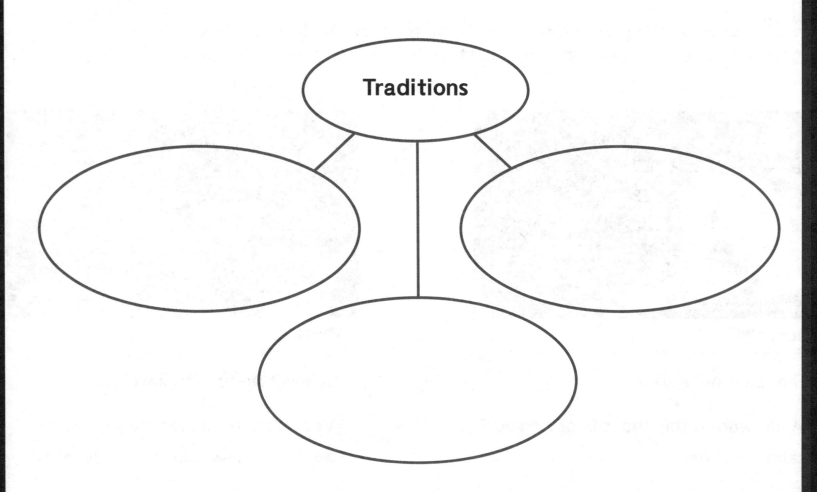

Traditions

Discuss how the woman shares. Use the words from the web. You can say:

The woman shares a tradition by _____.

People learn about _____.

More Vocabulary

Look at the picture and read the word. Then read the sentences.
Talk about the word with a partner. Write your own sentence.

nervous

The girl is **nervous**.

What word is the opposite of *nervous*?

calm   **fun**   **big**

When do you feel nervous?

I feel nervous when _____

_____.

share

Jack will **share** with the class.

What word or phrase means *share*?

see   **talk about**   **look at**

What do you like to share?

I like to share _____

_____.

Words and Phrases: Homophones *no* and *know*

The word *no* is the opposite of *yes*.

Can the girl play outside?

No, she cannot.

The word *know* means "to have information."

Who has the answer?

I **know** the answer.

COLLABORATE Talk with a partner. Look at the pictures. Read the sentences. Write the word that completes the sentence.

Can we go?

_____, you cannot go.

Know   No

I _____ the phone number.

know   no

COLLABORATE

1 Talk About It

Look at the picture. Read the title. Discuss what you see. Use these words.

**Peter   sad   house
grandmother**

Write about what you see.

The story is about _____

_____

_____.

Where is Peter walking?

Peter is walking _____

_____.

How does Peter feel?

Peter feels _____

_____.

Take notes as you read the text.

The Dream Catcher

Essential Question

? **What can traditions teach you about cultures?**

Read how Peter learns about his culture.

22

P eter walked home from school. Tears fell down his cheeks.

"What's wrong?" asked Peter's grandmother.

"I have to give a presentation at school. I have to talk about a family tradition. Our family has many **customs**. But I cannot think of one. Can you help me?" asked Peter.

Grandmother smiled. "Come with me," she said.

Richard Johnson

① Comprehension

Sequence

Reread the first paragraph. What happens in the beginning of the story?

In the beginning of the story,

Peter _____

_____.

② Sentence Structure Ⓐ Ⓒ Ⓣ

Reread the first paragraph. The pronoun *his* tells about the subject of the first sentence. Who does *his* refer to? Circle the word.

③ Specific Vocabulary Ⓐ Ⓒ Ⓣ

The word *customs* means "special things a group of people do." Reread the third paragraph. Why does Peter need to think of a custom?

Peter needs to _____

_____.

23

Text Evidence

1 Comprehension

Reread the first sentence in the first paragraph. Where does Grandmother walk? Underline the words.

2 Specific Vocabulary ⒶⒸⓉ

The word *center* means "the middle of something." What is in the center of the hoop? Write the word.

_____

COLLABORATE

3 Talk About It

What does Peter see when he opens the box?

Peter sees _____

_____.

How does Peter feel after he opens the box?

_____

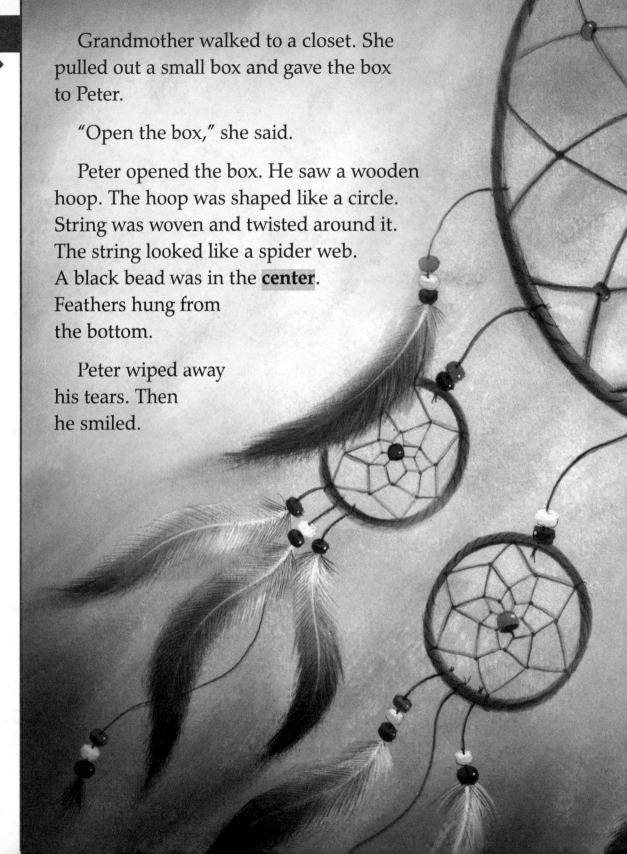

Grandmother walked to a closet. She pulled out a small box and gave the box to Peter.

"Open the box," she said.

Peter opened the box. He saw a wooden hoop. The hoop was shaped like a circle. String was woven and twisted around it. The string looked like a spider web. A black bead was in the **center**. Feathers hung from the bottom.

Peter wiped away his tears. Then he smiled.

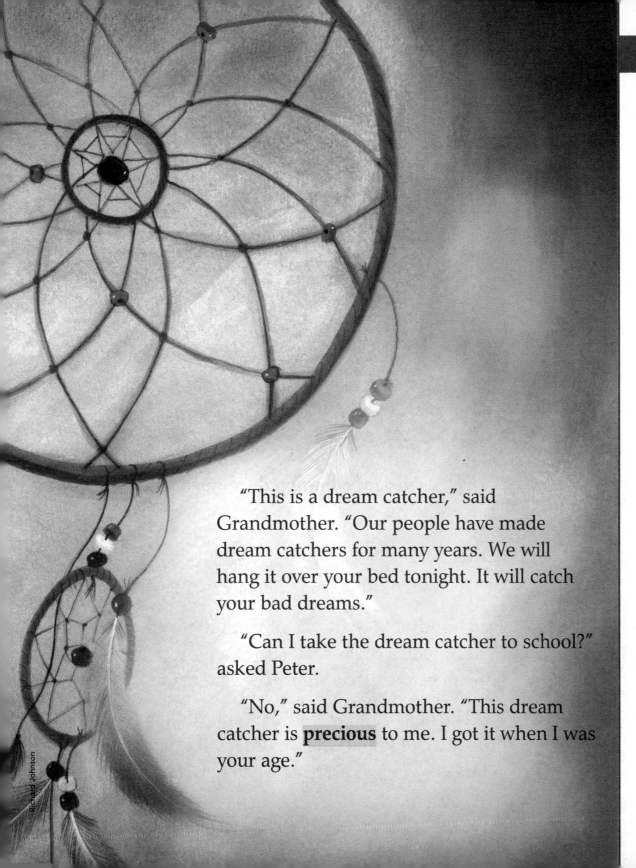

Richard Johnson

"This is a dream catcher," said Grandmother. "Our people have made dream catchers for many years. We will hang it over your bed tonight. It will catch your bad dreams."

"Can I take the dream catcher to school?" asked Peter.

"No," said Grandmother. "This dream catcher is **precious** to me. I got it when I was your age."

Text Evidence

1 **Sentence Structure** Ⓐ Ⓒ Ⓣ

Look at the second sentence in the first paragraph. Circle the subject. Then underline the words in the fourth sentence that tell what the subject does.

2 **Specific Vocabulary** Ⓐ Ⓒ Ⓣ

Reread the second sentence in the last paragraph. Another word for *precious* is *special*. Why is the dream catcher precious to Grandmother?

Grandmother got it when

_____

COLLABORATE

3 **Talk About It**

Grandmother does not want Peter to take the dream catcher to school. Explain why.

25

Text Evidence

1 Sentence Structure (A)(C)(T)

Reread the second paragraph. Circle the quotation marks. What words does Grandmother say? Underline the words.

2 Specific Vocabulary (A)(C)(T)

The word *gazed* means "looked at for a long time." What does Peter gaze at?

Peter gazes at _____

_____ .

COLLABORATE

3 Talk About It

Peter makes a plan. What is Peter's plan?

Peter makes a plan to _____

_____

_____ .

Peter felt sad. He wanted to show the dream catcher to his class.

"We can make you one," said Grandmother.

"I like that idea!" said Peter.

Grandmother and Peter worked together. They made a dream catcher. Peter **gazed** at the dream catcher that night. Then he made a plan.

The next day, Peter told Grandmother about the plan. "I know what to do. I will teach my class how to make a dream catcher," Peter said.

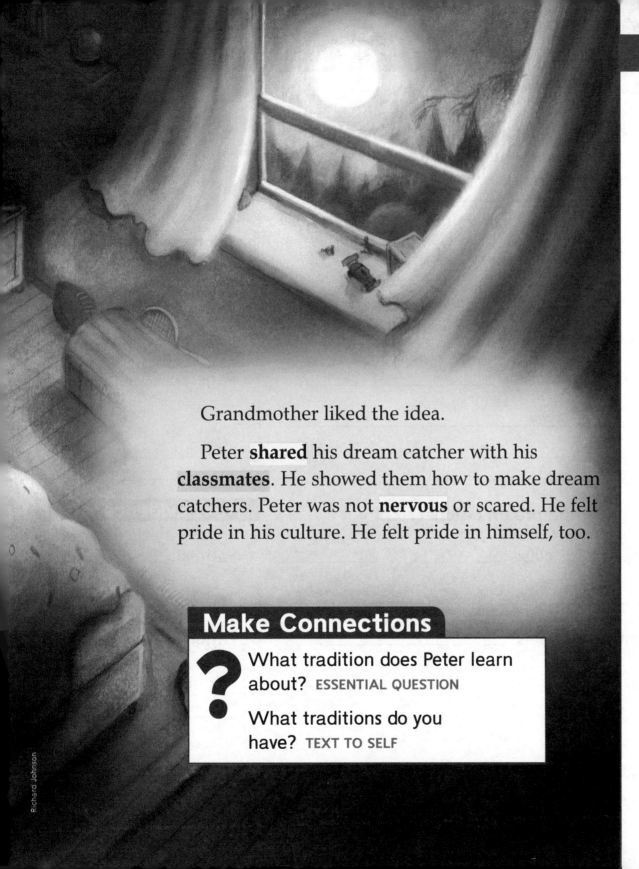

Grandmother liked the idea.

Peter **shared** his dream catcher with his **classmates**. He showed them how to make dream catchers. Peter was not **nervous** or scared. He felt pride in his culture. He felt pride in himself, too.

Make Connections

? What tradition does Peter learn about? ESSENTIAL QUESTION

What traditions do you have? TEXT TO SELF

1 **Specific Vocabulary** ACT

The word *classmates* is made up of two smaller words. Write the two words.

_____

What does Peter share with his classmates? Underline the words.

2 **Sentence Structure** ACT

Look at the third sentence. Underline the pronoun *them*. Circle the word that shows who *them* refers to.

COLLABORATE

3 **Talk About It**

Discuss Peter's feelings at the beginning and end of the story.

Peter feels _____ at the beginning of the story.

Peter feels _____ at the end of the story.

27

Richard Johnson

Respond to the Text

Partner Discussion Work with a partner. Read the questions about "The Dream Catcher." Show where you found text evidence. Write the page numbers. Then discuss what you learned.

Why does Peter need to find a family tradition?

I learned that Peter is sad because _____.

I read that Grandmother _____.

In the story, Peter and Grandmother _____

_____.

Text Evidence 🔍

Page(s): _____

Page(s): _____

Page(s): _____

What does Peter do with the dream catcher?

In the story, Peter teaches his class to _____

_____.

At the end of the story, Peter feels _____

_____.

Text Evidence 🔍

Page(s): _____

Page(s): _____

Group Discussion Present your answers to the group. Cite text evidence for your ideas. Listen and discuss the group's opinions.

Write Work with a partner. Look at your notes about "The Dream Catcher." Write your answer to the Essential Question. Use text evidence to support your answer. Use vocabulary words in your writing.

How does the dream catcher teach Peter about his culture?

Grandmother shows Peter _____.

Grandmother teaches Peter _____.

Peter teaches his class _____.

Peter feels _____.

Share Writing Present your writing to the class. Discuss their opinions. Talk about their ideas. Explain why you agree or disagree with their ideas. You can say:

I agree with _____.

That's a good comment, but _____.

Write to Sources

pages 22–27

Take Notes About the Text I took notes on the chart to respond to the prompt: *Add a descriptive paragraph to the story. Describe what happens in Peter's dream.*

Walter

> Grandmother showed Peter the dream catcher.

⬇

> Grandmother and Peter made a new dream catcher.

⬇

> Peter looked at the dream catcher that night.

30

Write About the Text **My descriptive paragraph tells what happens in Peter's dream.**

Student Model: *Narrative Text*

Peter had a dream. He saw a big spider! The spider chased Peter. Peter was scared. Then Peter saw his dream catcher. He ran to it. Peter touched it. The spider disappeared!

TALK ABOUT IT

Text Evidence

Draw a box around the sentence that tells how Peter feels. What does this sentence tell you about Peter's dream?

Grammar

Circle the past tense verb in the third sentence. Why does Walter use this verb?

Connect Ideas

Underline the last two sentences. How can you use the word *and* to combine the sentence and connect the ideas?

Your Turn

Add a paragraph to the end of the story. Write about what happens after Peter's school presentation.

>> *Go Digital*
Write your response online. Use your editing checklist.

31

TALK ABOUT IT

? **Essential Question**
How do people from different
cultures contribute to a community?

>> *Go Digital*

COLLABORATE **Who is in the picture? What are they doing? What are they sharing with the community? Write the words in the web.**

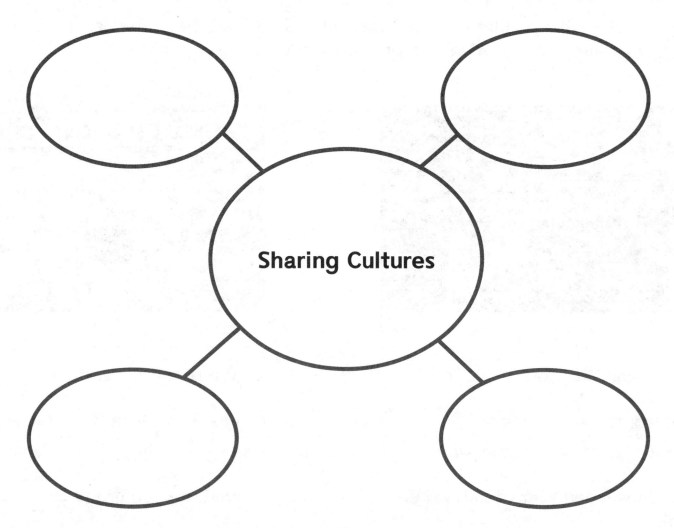

Sharing Cultures

Discuss what the children are sharing. Use the words from the web. You can say:

The children share _____.

The community will learn about _____ by _____.

More Vocabulary

Look at the picture and read the word. Then read the sentences. Talk about the word with a partner. Write your own sentence.

agreed

The girls **agreed** to play a game.

What words mean *agreed*?

said *no*   said *yes*   said *when*

What do you and your friends agree to do?

We agreed to _____

_____

_____.

proud

Pat is **proud** of her prize.

What word means the same as *proud*?

sad   happy   funny

What are you proud of?

I am proud of my _____

_____

_____.

Words and Phrases: Compound Words

cook + out = cookout

A *cookout* is a meal cooked and eaten outdoors.

Where is the cookout?

The **cookout** is in the yard.

sun + light = sunlight

Sunlight is light from the sun.

What do trees need?

Trees need **sunlight** to grow.

Talk with a partner. Look at the pictures. Read the sentences. Write the word that completes the sentence.

We are having a

_____ today.

The girls play in the

_____ .

1 Talk About It

Look at the picture. Read the title. Discuss what you see. Use these words.

family   girl   watering   plants

Write about what you see.

The text is about _____

_____

_____.

Who are the people?

The people are _____

_____.

What is the girl doing?

The girl is _____

_____.

Take notes as you read the text.

Room to Grow

Our new home in Portland

Essential Question

? How do people from different cultures contribute to a community?

Read how one family helps a community grow.

Spring in the City

I am Kiku Sato. My family and I moved to Portland in the spring. Portland is a big city.

Our new home had no yard. So Mama made an indoor garden. First she and Papa planted seeds in pots. Then they hung the pots. Next they **crammed** plants onto shelves. Our house had plants everywhere.

I was scared to start school. I was afraid because I did not have any friends. But I soon met Jill. We became best friends. Jill spent much time at my house.

Map of Oregon

OREGON

PENDLETON

PORTLAND

★ SALEM

EUGENE

ASHLAND

N
W   E
S

KEY
• CITY
★ CAPITAL
~ RIVER

(flowers) Japack/amanaimagesRF/Corbis; (bkgd) Wetzel and Company; (c) Margaret Lindmark

Text Evidence

❶ Comprehension

Sequence

Mama and Papa make an indoor garden. What do they do first? Underline the sentence. Circle the sequence word.

❷ Specific Vocabulary Ⓐ Ⓒ Ⓣ

The word *crammed* means "put many things in a small space." Reread the second paragraph. What sentence shows what *crammed* means? Underline it.

❸ Sentence Structure Ⓐ Ⓒ Ⓣ

Look at the last paragraph. The pronoun *we* refers to two people. Who does *we* refer to? Write the words.

_____

_____

Text Evidence

1 Specific Vocabulary **A C T**

The word *visit* means "to come and see." Underline who visits. What do they see?

_____ and _____ see _____

_____.

2 Sentence Structure **A C T**

Reread the second sentence in the first paragraph. What word adds a detail about the plants? Circle the word.

COLLABORATE

3 Talk About It

What do Jill and her mother do during their visit?

Jill and her mother _____

_____

_____.

An idea for a garden

One day Jill and her mother came to **visit** Papa, Mama, and me. They saw our beautiful plants. "Jill told me about your indoor garden," her mother said.

We all sat down, and Mama made tea. First Mama put tea in a bowl. Then she added hot water. She gave the bowl to Jill's mother and bowed.

Mama's special tea bowls

38

Grandmother in Japan

(flowers) Japack/amanaimagesRF/Corbis; (bkgd) Wetzel and Company; (c) Margaret Lindmark

"My mother taught me many things," said Mama. "I learned to make tea. And I learned to plant a Japanese garden. I learned to use a small space."

Jill's mom smiled. "Can you help us?" she asked. "Our community wants to plant a garden. Our **plot** of land is small. There is so much we want to grow."

Papa looked at Mama. They bowed.

"Yes, we'll help," they **agreed**.

1 Sentence Structure Ⓐ Ⓒ Ⓣ

Reread the second sentence in the first paragraph. Circle the subject of the sentence. Underline the words that tell what the subject does.

2 Specific Vocabulary Ⓐ Ⓒ Ⓣ

The word *plot* means "a piece of land." Reread the second paragraph. What will the community do with the plot? Circle the words that tell you.

COLLABORATE

3 Talk About It

How can Kiku's mother help the community?

Kiku's mother knows how to

_____.

Kiku's mother can _____

_____

_____.

1 **Comprehension**

Sequence

Look at the second paragraph. Underline what happens first. Circle the sequence word.

Kiku and her parents filled

_____.

2 **Sentence Structure** **ACT**

Reread the second paragraph. Where does the family put the tallest box? Circle the words that tell you. Where is the shortest box? Underline words that tell you.

COLLABORATE

3 **Talk About It**

Discuss why the family makes short and tall boxes.

The family makes short and tall

boxes because _____

_____.

A Garden Grows

We had a meeting with the community. Some people brought seeds, tools, and dirt. The next day we met and started our garden.

First, Papa built boxes. Next, we filled them with dirt. We put the tallest box close to the wall. The shortest box was in the front. "Now all the plants will get sunlight," Mama said.

Papa builds boxes

Jill and I plant seeds

Then, we made a rock path. Finally, we planted the seeds.

Jill and I worked in the garden all summer. Our garden had many vegetables. We picked them at the end of the summer. We had enough to have a cookout. Everyone thanked Mama and Papa for their help. I was so **proud**.

Look! We picked these!

Make Connections

? How did Kiku's family help the community? What parts of their culture did they share? ESSENTIAL QUESTION

How can your family contribute to your community? TEXT TO SELF

Text Evidence

1 **Comprehension**

Sequence

Look at the first paragraph. What happens last? Underline the sentence. Circle the sequence word.

2 **Sentence Structure** **A C T**

Reread the second paragraph. When do Jill and Kiku work in the garden? Circle the words that tell you. When do they pick the vegetables?

They pick the vegetables _____

_____.

COLLABORATE

3 **Talk About It**

Why is Kiku proud?

The family helped make _____

_____.

Respond to the Text

Partner Discussion Work with a partner. Read the questions about "Room to Grow." Show where you found text evidence. Write the page numbers. Then discuss what you learned.

What does Kiku tell us about her culture?

I read that Kiku's family makes _____.

Then Mama serves _____ to _____.

According to Kiku, Mama knows how to _____

_____.

Text Evidence

Page(s): _____

Page(s): _____

Page(s): _____

How do Kiku and her family help the community?

Jill's mother asks Kiku's family _____.

According to Kiku, her family makes _____.

At the end of the summer, _____

_____.

Text Evidence

Page(s): _____

Page(s): _____

Page(s): _____

Group Discussion Present your ideas to the group. Cite text evidence for your ideas. Listen to and discuss the group's opinions.

Write Work with a partner. Look at your notes about "Room to Grow." Write your answer to the Essential Question. Use text evidence to support your answer. Use vocabulary words in your writing.

COLLABORATE

> **How do Kiku and her family contribute to the community?**
>
> Mama knows how to _____.
>
> Jill's mother asks _____.
>
> Kiku's family shows the community how to _____
>
> a _____.
>
> The community grows _____ and has a _____.

Share Writing Present your writing to the class. Discuss their opinions. Talk about their ideas. Explain why you agree or disagree with their ideas. You can say:

COLLABORATE

I think your ideas are _____.

I do not agree because _____.

Write to Sources

pages 36–41

Take Notes About the Text I took notes about the text on this chart. I will answer the question: *What point does the author make in this selection?*

Gina

People bring seeds and tools to the garden.

⬇

Mama and Papa help the community make a garden.

⬇

Jill and Kiku pick vegetables for a cookout.

Write About the Text I used my notes. I wrote an informative paragraph. It explains the author's point.

Student Model: *Informative Text*

The author makes a point. People can work together and do a lot. First, Mama and Papa help the community. They show people how to make a garden. People work together. Finally, Jill and Kiku pick many vegetables. They have a cookout!

TALK ABOUT IT

COLLABORATE

Text Evidence

Circle a sentence that comes from the notes. Which word in the sentence tells when it happens?

Grammar

Circle the word *vegetables*. What does the *-s* in the word tell you?

Connect Ideas

Underline two sentences about how Mama and Papa help the community. How can you combine the sentences?

Your Turn

COLLABORATE

How does Kiku's community work together? Use text evidence in your writing.

>> *Go Digital*
Write your response online. Use your editing checklist.

45

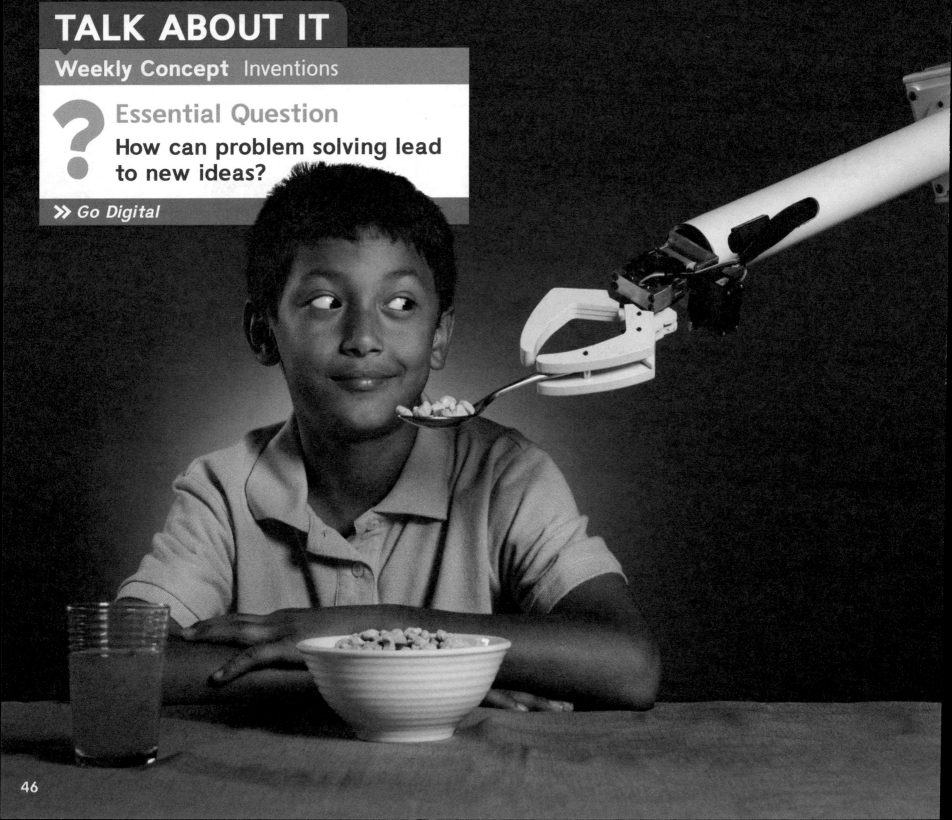

TALK ABOUT IT

Weekly Concept Inventions

? Essential Question
How can problem solving lead to new ideas?

>> *Go Digital*

COLLABORATE

What is the boy looking at? What is the robot doing? Is this a good idea? Write the words in the web.

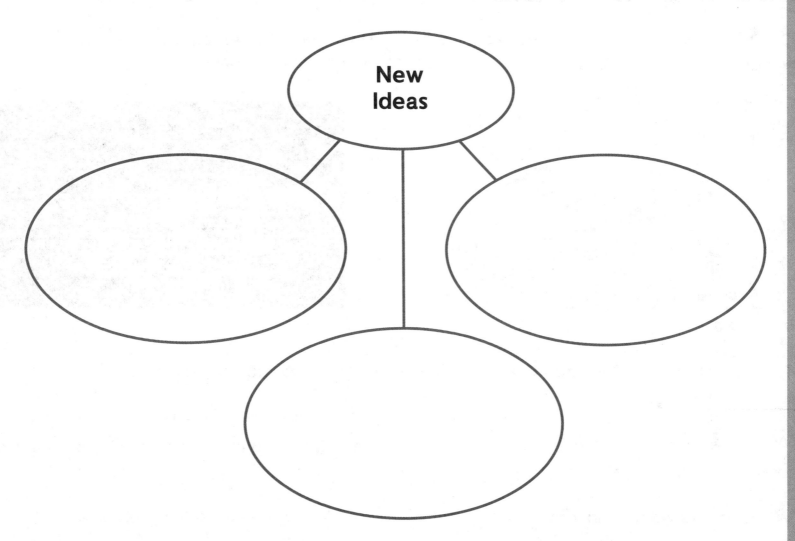

New Ideas

Discuss the new idea in the picture. What problem does the robot solve? Use the words from the web. You can say:

The robot feeds the boy _____.

This is a new idea because _____.

More Vocabulary

COLLABORATE

Look at the picture and read the word. Then read the sentences. Talk about the word with a partner. Write your own sentence.

invented

The Wright brothers **invented** the first airplane.

What word means *invented*?

wore   made   saw

What do you want to invent?

I want to invent _____

_____.

solved

Jill **solved** the problem.

What does the word *solve* mean?

like   get an answer   work with a friend

When do you solve problems?

I solve problems when _____

_____.

Words and Phrases: Regular Plurals

The word *cow* means "one cow."

What is in the field?

One **cow** is in the field.

The word *cows* means "more than one cow."

What is in the field?

The **cows** are in the field.

COLLABORATE

Talk with a partner. Look at the pictures. Read the sentences. Write the word that completes the sentence.

The _____ are running.

girl   girls

Sam has a _____.

dog   dogs

COLLABORATE

❶ Talk About It

Look at the picture. Read the title. Discuss what you see. Use these words.

woman   invented   long   ago

Write about what you see.

The biography is about _____

_____

_____.

When does the biography take place?

The biography takes place _____

_____.

What did the woman do?

The woman _____

_____.

Take notes as you read the text.

50

Mary Anderson's
GREAT
INVENTION

Essential Question

? **How can problem solving lead to new ideas?**

Read about how someone solved a problem and invented something new.

Think about a ride in a bus or a car. It is not the same today as it was long ago. The first cars were slow. Cars did not even have windshield wipers!

What happened when it rained? Drivers used an onion. They **rubbed** the onion on the windshield. An onion has oil in it. The oil kept off the rain. Nothing else worked. Then a woman named Mary Anderson **solved** the problem.

Mailene Laugesen

1 Sentence Structure A C T

An exclamation mark shows a strong feeling. Reread the first paragraph. Circle the exclamation mark.

The exclamation mark shows the author's strong feelings

about _____.

2 Specific Vocabulary A C T

The word *rub* means "move something back and forth." Why did drivers rub an onion on their windshields? Underline the sentences that tell you.

COLLABORATE

3 Talk About It

Look at the picture and reread the text. How were cars long ago different from cars today?

Long ago, cars did not have

_____.

Text Evidence

① Specific Vocabulary ⒶⒸⓉ

A blanket is a large piece of cloth. It covers something. Read sentence four in the first paragraph. What was like a blanket? Underline the word. Where was the blanket?

The blanket was on _____

_____.

② Comprehension

Cause and Effect

Read the first paragraph. Why did Mary ride in a streetcar?

Mary rode in a streetcar

because _____.

COLLABORATE

③ Talk About It

What problem did streetcar drivers have?

The streetcar drivers could not

see when _____.

It Started with Snow

It was 1902. Mary traveled to New York City. It was a cold winter day. The snow was a white **blanket** on the ground. Mary was cold and wet. She wanted to be warm and dry, so she rode in a streetcar.

Mary watched the snow fall. It piled up on the windshield. The driver could not see. So he pushed open the windshield. Snow blew in his face. Soon his face looked very cold.

Other cars stopped, too. The drivers hopped out. They wiped off their windshields. As a result, traffic moved slowly.

The Next Step

Mary thought about this problem. Drivers could not clean their windshields. Then Mary had an idea.

Mary drew her **idea** on paper. She added notes. And she learned what drivers needed. Then Mary **invented** a wiper for windshields. A driver could use it from inside the car.

Mary looked at her drawing. The invention was simple. Mary hoped that it was easy to use. She wanted to help drivers.

Mary Anderson's Windshield Wiper

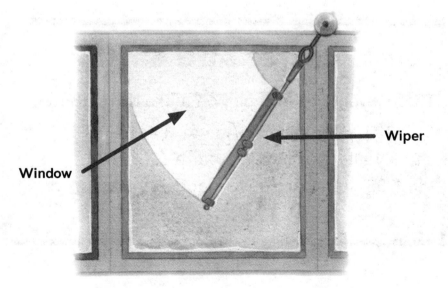

This diagram shows Mary Anderson's invention.

Malene Laugesen

1 Sentence Structure A C T

Reread the first paragraph. Circle the subject in the first sentence. Underline the words that tell what the subject does.

2 Specific Vocabulary A C T

Look at the word *idea*. An idea is a thought someone has. What was Mary's idea?

Mary's idea was _____

_____.

COLLABORATE

3 Talk About It

What did Mary do after she had an idea?

First, Mary _____

and _____.

Then she _____.

1 Sentence Structure A C T

Reread the third sentence in the first paragraph. Circle the noun *handle*. Underline the words that tell where the handle is.

2 Comprehension

Cause and Effect

Reread the second paragraph. At first, people did not use Mary's wipers. Circle the words that tell the reason.

COLLABORATE

3 Talk About It

Why did windshield wipers help drivers?

Windshield wipers helped

drivers because _____

_____.

Soon the wiper was ready to test. So Mary placed a wiper on a windshield. The driver moved a handle inside the car. The handle moved a blade across the glass. It worked! Mary was happy with her invention.

Solving the Problem

At first, people did not use Mary's wiper. What was the reason? Most people did not own cars.

More people had cars by 1913. Those cars needed wipers. So the windshield wipers began to sell. Mary's idea made driving safer. It also made driving easier.

Better and Safer

These inventions also helped make driving safer.

- In 1885, people began to use seat belts. Today all riders in cars wear a seat belt.
- In 1938, turn signals were added to cars.

Make Connections

? Mary Anderson solved a problem. What new idea did the solution lead to? ESSENTIAL QUESTION

What inventions make your life better? TEXT TO SELF

Malene Laugesen

Text Evidence

1 **Comprehension**

Cause and Effect

Reread "Better and Safer." What happened to driving when people began to use seat belts?

Using seat belts made driving

_____.

COLLABORATE

2 **Talk About It**

Discuss how Mary Anderson invented the windshield wiper. Use details from the text.

Mary Anderson saw _____

_____

Mary drew _____

_____.

Mary invented _____

_____.

Respond to the Text

Partner Discussion Work with a partner. Read the questions about "Mary Anderson's Great Invention." Show where you found text evidence. Write the page numbers. Then discuss what you learned.

What problem did Mary see?

I read that long ago cars did not have _____.

On snowy days, drivers had to _____.

According to the author, drivers were not able to see because

_____.

Text Evidence 🔍
Page(s): _____
Page(s): _____
Page(s): _____

How did Mary Anderson solve this problem?

I learned that Mary Anderson invented a _____.

Mary's invention _____.

People began to use Mary's invention _____.

Text Evidence 🔍
Page(s): _____
Page(s): _____
Page(s): _____

Group Discussion Present your answers to the group. Cite text evidence for your ideas. Listen to and discuss the group's opinions about your answers.

Write Work with a partner. Look at your notes about "Mary Anderson's Great Invention." Write your answer to the Essential Question. Use text evidence to support your answer. Use vocabulary words in your writing.

How did Mary Anderson solve a problem and invent something new?

Long ago drivers could not _____

_____.

Based on the text, Mary invented _____.

The windshield wiper helped drivers _____.

Share Writing Present your writing to the class. Discuss their opinions. Talk about their ideas. Explain why you agree or disagree with their ideas. You can say:

I think your idea is _____, but _____.

I do not agree because _____.

Write to Sources

pages 50–55

Take Notes About the Text I took notes about the text on the chart to answer the questions: *What problem did Mary want to solve? How did she solve it? Explain using text evidence.*

David

Problem: Snow piled up on drivers' windshields.
Drivers could not see.

First, Mary drew her idea on paper.

Next, Mary invented a wiper for windshields.

Finally, a driver tested the wiper.

Write About the Text My informative paragraph explains the problem and how Mary solved it.

Student Model: *Informative Text*

The streetcar drivers had a problem. Snow piled up on their windshields. The drivers were not able to see. Mary wanted to solve the problem. First, Mary drew her idea on paper. Next, Mary invented a wiper for windshields. Finally, a driver tested the wiper. It worked!

TALK ABOUT IT

COLLABORATE

Text Evidence
Draw a box around the seventh sentence. Which word shows that this happened last?

Grammar
Circle the sentence that tells what Mary did first. Which words tell what Mary did?

Connect Ideas
Underline two sentences that explain the problem. How can you use the word *so* to connect the ideas?

Your Turn

COLLABORATE

Why do people think of ideas for inventions? Use evidence from the text to support your answer.

>> Go Digital
Write your response online. Use your editing checklist.

59

TALK ABOUT IT

Weekly Concept Landmarks

? **Essential Question**
How do landmarks help us
understand our country's story?

>> *Go Digital*

What landmark do you see? Why is it important? Write the words in the web.

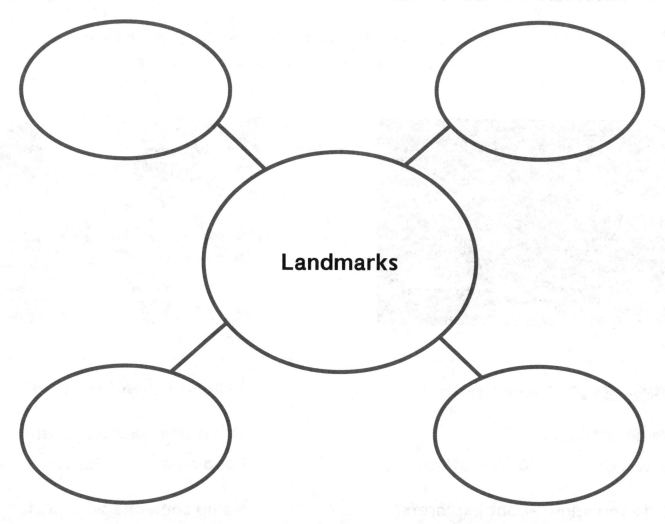

Landmarks

Talk about the landmark. What does it show? Why is it important? Use the words from the web. You can say:

The landmark is a _____.

Many people _____.

The landmark shows _____.

More Vocabulary

Look at the picture and read the word. Then read the sentences.
Talk about the word with a partner. Write your own sentence.

explorers

The **explorers** go to a new place.

Where do *explorers* go?

to the woods**to food stores**

What do you know about explorers?

Explorers are people who _____

_____

_____.

protect

Helmets **protect** our heads.

What does *protect* mean?

keep safe**hurt****like**

Name someone who protects people.

A _____ protects people by

_____

_____.

Words and Phrases: Prepositions *across* and *to*

The word *across* means "from one side to the other."

Where did the horse run?

The horse ran **across** the field.

The word *to* tells where.

Where are they going?

They are going **to** the beach.

Talk with a partner. Look at the pictures. Read the sentences. Write the word that completes the sentence.

The students walk _____ the street.

across   to

We are going _____ school.

across   to

COLLABORATE

1 Talk About It

Look at the picture. Read the title. Discuss what you see. Use these words.

**beautiful   cliffs   canyon
nature**

Write about what you see.

This text is about _____

_____.

What do you see in the photograph?

The Grand Canyon has _____

_____.

Why is the Grand Canyon a natural beauty?

It is a natural beauty because

_____.

Take notes as you read the text.

Essential Question

? **How do landmarks help us understand our country's story?**

Read about what one landmark teaches us.

A Natural Beauty

The Grand Canyon is an important landmark in the United States. It is huge! It was carved by the Colorado River. And it stretches across four states.

Exploring the Canyon

Many **tourists** take trips to the Grand Canyon each year. People come from different places to hike the trails. They take boat rides down the river. They look at the beautiful cliffs.

Nature lovers visit the Grand Canyon, too. They come to look for animals. They peek at plants. They spot eagles. They spy snakes. Some visitors even see bats. And some come to learn about the Canyon's history.

Kristy-Anne Glubish/Design Pics

Text Evidence

1 Specific Vocabulary Ⓐ🄲Ⓣ

The word *discover* means "to see or find something for the first time." What word means almost the same as *discover*? Write the word.

_____

2 Sentence Structure Ⓐ🄲Ⓣ

Reread the second paragraph. The pronouns *they* and *their* refer to a group of people. Who do *they* and *their* refer to? Write the name of the group.

_____

_____

COLLABORATE

3 Talk About It

Why are the very old rocks in the canyon important?

The rocks show _____

_____

Canyon History

American explorers **discovered** the Grand Canyon in 1857. The **explorers** found Native Americans there. One group was the Ancient Pueblo people.

This is a cliff house. Ancient Pueblo people lived in it.

The Ancient Pueblo lived in the canyon for almost one thousand years. They were farmers and hunters. Parts of their homes are still standing.

Scientists found very old rocks in the Grand Canyon. These rocks tell how the canyon was formed.

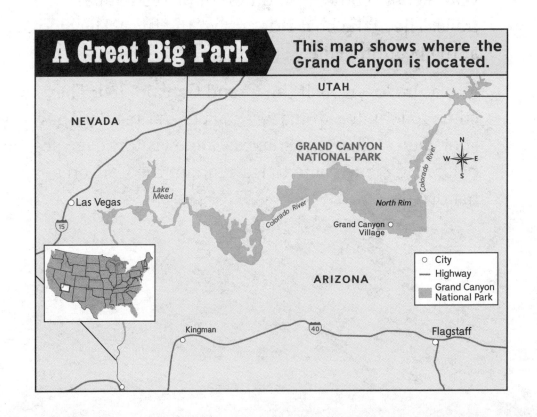

A Great Big Park

This map shows where the Grand Canyon is located.

UTAH

NEVADA

GRAND CANYON NATIONAL PARK

Colorado River

Lake Mead

Las Vegas

North Rim

Grand Canyon Village

15

City
Highway
Grand Canyon National Park

ARIZONA

Kingman

40

Flagstaff

(tl) © Canyon Florey/Aurora Photos/Corbis; (bl) Mapping Specialists, Ltd. (r) Matt Dil/Flickr/Getty Images

A Landmark

President Theodore Roosevelt visited the Grand Canyon. He saw that it was beautiful. He said it was a special place. In 1919, the government **declared** that the Canyon was a national park. Now the land is **protected**. People cannot build homes there. Now all people can enjoy the Grand Canyon.

Protect the Canyon

We must take care of the Grand Canyon. It is a landmark. How can we help? We have to follow the rules when we visit. Animals are safe there. People should not touch the wildlife. Rivers must be kept clean.

There is still a lot to learn about this beautiful landmark. It is important that we protect it.

Make Connections

 How does the Grand Canyon teach us about America's story? ESSENTIAL QUESTION

What is most interesting about the Grand Canyon's history? Why? TEXT TO SELF

Bighorn sheep live in the Grand Canyon.

Text Evidence

1 Specific Vocabulary Ⓐ Ⓒ Ⓣ

The word *declare* means "to tell people something." What did the government declare in 1919?

The government declared

_____.

2 Comprehension

Main Idea and Key Details

Reread the first paragraph in "Protect the Canyon." People must take care of the Grand Canyon. Which key details support this main idea? Underline two key details.

COLLABORATE

3 Talk About It

What can people do to protect the Grand Canyon?

People can protect the Grand Canyon by _____.

Respond to the Text

Partner Discussion Work with a partner. Read the questions about "A Natural Beauty." Show where you found text evidence. Write the page numbers. Then discuss what you learned.

Why is the Grand Canyon a landmark?

Tourists visit the canyon because _____.

Based on the text, explorers found _____.

The author writes that scientists found _____

_____.

Text Evidence 🔍

Page(s): _____

Page(s): _____

Page(s): _____

Why should we protect the Grand Canyon?

President Roosevelt visited _____ and _____.

The Grand Canyon became a landmark _____.

Based on the text, we protect _____.

Text Evidence 🔍

Page(s): _____

Page(s): _____

Page(s): _____

Group Discussion Present your answers to the group. Cite text evidence for your ideas. Listen to and discuss the group's opinions.

Write Work with a partner. Look at your notes about "A Natural Beauty." Write your answer to the Essential Question. Use text evidence to support your answer. Use vocabulary words in your writing.

How does the Grand Canyon help us understand our country's story?

Tourists visit _____ because _____

_____.

Explorers discovered _____.

Scientists found _____ that show _____

_____.

The Grand Canyon became _____

_____.

Share Writing Present your writing to the class. Discuss their opinions. Talk about their ideas. Explain why you agree or disagree with their ideas. You can say:

I think your idea is _____.

I do not agree because _____.

Write to Sources

Patrick

Take Notes About the Text I took notes about the text on this idea web to answer the question: *In your opinion, does the author show that the Grand Canyon is an important landmark? Use text evidence in your answer.*

pages 64–67

The canyon stretches across four states.

Many animals live in the canyon.

The author shows that the Grand Canyon is an important landmark.

Some people visit to see nature.

Other people visit to learn about the canyon's history.

Write About the Text I used notes from my idea web to write an opinion about the text.

Student Model: *Opinion*

This author is good at telling about the Grand Canyon! He shows that the canyon is an important landmark. The canyon reaches across four states. Many animals live there. Some people come to see nature. Other people come to learn about the canyon's history. These details show why the Grand Canyon is important.

TALK ABOUT IT

Text Evidence
Draw a box around the first sentence. Why does Patrick use an exclamation point in this sentence?

Grammar
Circle the fourth sentence. What word can you add to describe the animals?

Connect Ideas
Underline the sentences that tell why people come to the park. How can you use the word *but* to connect the ideas?

Your Turn

Why should we protect the Grand Canyon? Use details from the text to support your opinion.

>> Go Digital
Write your response online. Use your editing checklist.